Easy Duets for Cello

MB99813

By Costel Puscoiu

© 2009 BY MEL BAY PUBLICATIONS, INC., PACIFIC, MO 63069.
ALL RIGHTS RESERVED. INTERNATIONAL COPYRIGHT SECURED. B.M.I. MADE AND PRINTED IN U.S.A.
No part of this publication may be reproduced in whole or in part, or stored in a retrieval system, or transmitted in any form
or by any means, electronic, mechanical, photocopy, recording, or otherwise, without written permission of the publisher.

Visit us on the Web at www.melbay.com or www.billsmusicshelf.com

Contents

Ode to Joy	Ludwig van Beethoven	3
Anti Ti	Costel Puscoiu	4
Air	Wolfgang Amadeus Mozart	5
Barcarolle	Costel Puscoiu	6
Oh, Susanna	American Folk Song	7
The Green Leaf of the Jasmine	Romanian Folk Song	8
I say Adieu	Old Dutch Song	9
Little Song	Costel Puscoiu	10
The Volga Boatmen's Song	Russian Folk Song	11
Slowly	Costel Puscoiu	12
Gavotte	George Friedrich Händel	13
Burlesque	Leopold Mozart	14
Ostinato	Costel Puscoiu	15
Greensleeves	Old English Song	16
Dance from Moldavia	Romanian Folk Song	17
Children's Song	Bulgarian Folk Song	18
Gavotte	George Friedrich Händel	19
Because We Are Cheerful	Valentin Rathgeber	20
Musz i Denn	German Folk Song	21
Tiribomba	Italian Folk Song	22
March	George Friedrich Händel	23
Rondino	Jean Philippe Rameau	24
El Condor Pasa	Bolivian Folk Song	25
Tambourin	Jean Philippe Rameau	26
Coloured Socks	Macedonian Folk Song	27
Galoppa, Galoppa	Chilian Folk Song	28
Joy to the World	George Friedrich Händel	29
Dialogue	Costel Puscoiu	30
Hungarian Dance	Johannes Brahms	31
Greeting	Costel Puscoiu	32
Merry Widow Waltz	Franz Lehar	33
El Cacimbo	Chilian Folk Song	34
Pavane	Gabriel Fauré	35
Yerakina	Grecian Folk Song	36
El Humahuaqueno	Bolivian Folk Song	37
Theme from "Swan Lake"	Peter Ilici Tchaikovsky	38
Rejoicing	George Friedrich Händel	39

Ode to Joy

Ludwig van Beethoven

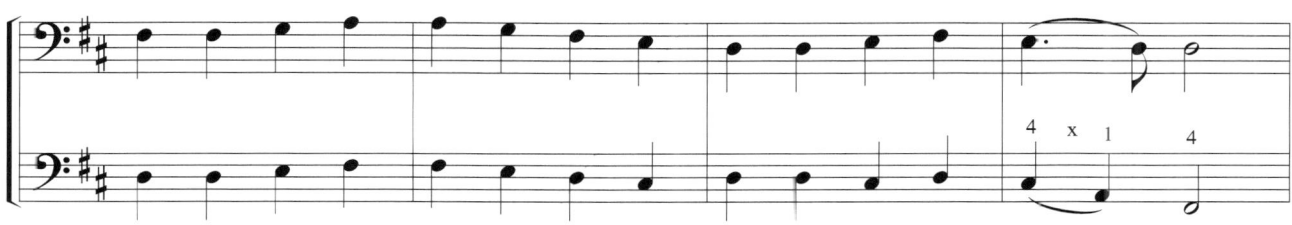

Anti Ti

Andantino

Costel Puscoiu

Air

Wolfgang Amadeus Mozart

Barcarolle

Allegro
Costel Puscoiu

Oh, Susanna

The Green Leaf of the Jasmine

Allegretto   Romanian Folk Song

I Say Adieu

Moderato Old Dutch Song

Little Song

Costel Puscoiu

The Volga Boatmen's Song

Slowly

Andantino Costel Puscoiu

Gavotte

Moderato
George Friedrich Handel

Burlesque

Ostinato

Greensleeves

Andante
Old English Song

Dance from Moldavia

Children's Song

Gavotte

George Friedrich Handel

Because We Are Cheerful

Musz I Denn

Tiribomba

Allegro
Italian Folk Song

March

Maestoso
George Friedrich Handel

Rondino

Jean Philippe Rameau

El Condor Pasa

Moderato   Bolivian Folk Song

Tambourin

Colored Socks

Allegro giocoso

Macedonian Folk Song

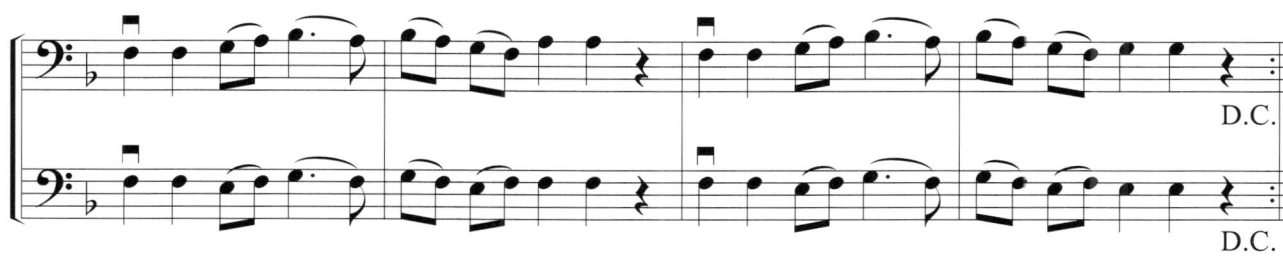

Galoppa, Galoppa

Allegretto   Chilian Folk Song

Joy to the World

George Friedrich Handel

Dialogue

Costel Puscoiu

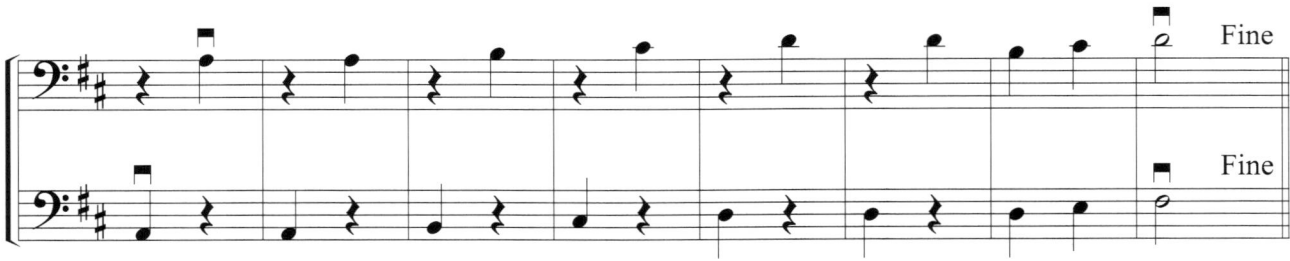

Hungarian Dance

Greeting

Allegretto giocoso

Costel Puscoiu

Merry Widow Waltz

Franz Lehar

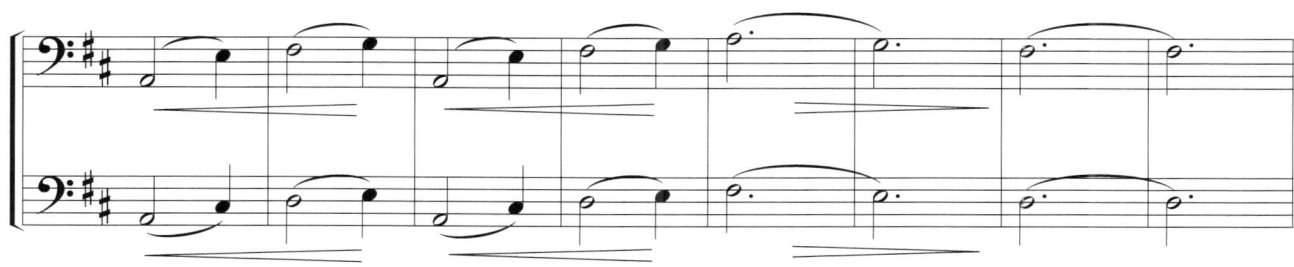
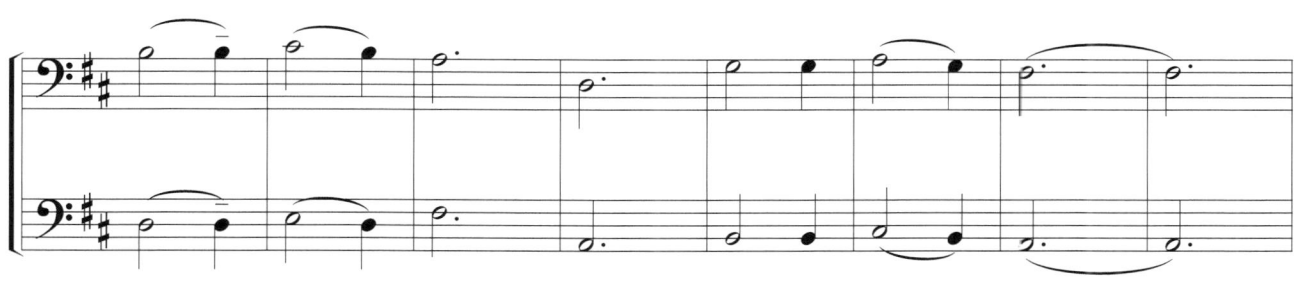
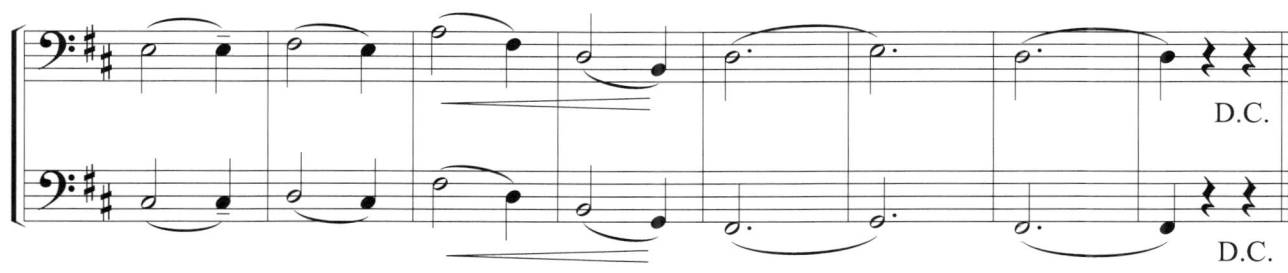

El Cachimbo

Allegretto   Chilian Folk Song

Pavane

Andantino cantabile
Gabriel Faure

Yerakina

El Humahuaqueno

Allegretto   Bolivian Folk Song

Theme from "Swan Lake"

Peter Ilici Tchaikovsky

Rejoicing

Allegro

George Friedrich Handel

8714541R0

Made in the USA
Charleston, SC
08 July 2011